the guide to

Handraising Kittens

Susan Easterly

Photo: Weems S. Hutto

© T.F.H. Publications, Inc.

Distributed in the UNITED STATES to the Pet Trade by T.F.H. Publications, Inc., 1 TFH Plaza, Neptune City, NJ 07753; on the Internet at www.tfh.com; in CANADA by Rolf C. Hagen Inc., 3225 Sartelon St., Montreal, Quebec H4R 1E8; Pet Trade by H & L Pet Supplies Inc., 27 Kingston Crescent, Kitchener, Ontario N2B 2T6; in ENGLAND by T.F.H. Publications, PO Box 74, Havant PO9 5TT; in AUSTRALIA AND THE SOUTH PACIFIC by T.F.H. (Australia), Pty. Ltd., Box 149, Brookvale 2100 N.S.W., Australia; in NEW ZEALAND by Brooklands Aquarium Ltd., 5 McGiven Drive, New Plymouth, RD1 New Zealand; in SOUTH AFRICA by Rolf C. Hagen S.A. (PTY.) LTD., P.O. Box 201199, Durban North 4016, South Africa; in JAPAN by T.F.H. Publications. Published by T.F.H. Publications, Inc.

**MANUFACTURED IN THE
UNITED STATES OF AMERICA
BY T.F.H. PUBLICATIONS, INC.**

Contents

Introduction to Handraising Kittens 3

First Aid for Kittens 6

Fostering Kittens 13

Hand-Feeding Kittens 18

Weaning Your Kitten 30

Sense and Sociability 34

Special Needs of Single Kittens 38

The Sick Kitten 44

Taming Feral Kittens 50

Letting Go of the Orphan Kitten 56

Appendix 60

Index 64

Photo: Isabelle Francais

Introduction to Handraising Kittens

You may find them in a box by the side of a road, under a porch, or in the bushes. You may hear a tiny cry in your garage or in a basket left on your doorstep. Neonatal kittens have only a tenuous hold on life, because they are completely dependent on their mother for warmth, nutrition, and protection. Without her, they become orphans that cannot survive for long. Orphan kittens are generally described as kittens deprived of their natural mother when they are younger than six to eight weeks old. Kittens become orphans when their mother dies or becomes ill. She may also abandon or reject one or more kittens in her litter. This, of course, is where you come in. You may turn out to be the hero, or the savior, of an orphan kitten's life.

Yes, you can successfully handraise orphan kittens to healthy adulthood. No one should ever suggest, however, that it is going to be easy. On the contrary, taking the place of a mother cat is daunting, whether you find just one tiny abandoned waif or a litter of four small kittens. What comes naturally to a mother cat must be accomplished under less-than-perfect, manmade conditions. In addition to handling the nitty-gritty basics of kitten care, for example, you will also need to teach orphan kittens how to become well-socialized cats. The truth is, orphan kittens present special challenges that require your

Neonatal kittens have only a tenuous hold on life, because they are completely dependent on their mother for warmth, nutrition, and protection.
Photo: Ginger S. Buck

Whether you find them in a box by the side of the road or in a basket left on your doorstep, orphaned kittens need your help to survive. *Photo: Isabelle Francais*

commitment, compassion and, at least at first, round-the-clock attention.

Fortunately, reaching for this book can help. *The Guide to Handraising Kittens* is dedicated to providing information about caring for kittens during their first critical weeks of life, including their nutritional, medical, and psychological needs. The following chapters can help guide you through the sometimes bumpy process of a kitten's first weeks. For example, kittens need the right formula to fill their tummies and furnish the right amount of nutrients, but they also need to meet timely social requirements to nourish their mental development. The unique challenges of feral, or wild, kittens are also presented in this book, as well as a chapter on letting your kittens go to new loving homes in the best possible way.

Be sure to use this book in conjunction with a licensed veterinarian who is willing to help you deal with the unique problems and situations you may encounter. He or she can offer critical emotional support for you and make a lifesaving difference to your kittens. If your kittens are not thriving or seem ill or weak, be sure to contact your veterinarian immediately.

No doubt—getting orphan kittens past their first critical weeks brings a deep sense of satisfaction and joy. I guarantee you that it will be one of the most rewarding adventures you ever embark on. Sometimes, though, despite your best efforts and long hours spent doing all the right things, orphan kittens do not thrive. In most cases, it is important to realize that a kitten's death is not your fault, especially if you have done everything possible to help her survive. Realize that it is okay to grieve but not to blame yourself. Instead, focus on the warmth, care, and comfort you have given your kitten, and remember that you made a loving difference in a tiny life.

Helping tiny, fragile babies grow into big, bright-eyed, boisterous kittens is one of the most rewarding experiences any cat lover could have. *Photo: Beverly Adams*

First Aid
for Kittens

People who love cats just seem to find them. Is this fate or coincidence? Wherever or however orphan kittens appear in your life, you won't have time to debate the question—you must act quickly to save their lives. Nearly helpless at birth, kittens depend on their mother to take care of every need. This chapter describes what you'll need to do if you suddenly become "Mom" to one or more orphan kittens.

WHAT SHOULD I DO FIRST?

If you discover a litter of tiny kittens outdoors, your first thought may be to gather them up and take them home immediately. Stop! Before you jump in to

If you discover a litter of tiny kittens outdoors, be sure to determine if they are truly orphaned or if their mother is nearby. *Photo: Ron Reagan*

"save" them, make sure the litter you find is truly orphaned. It's not uncommon for mother cats to leave their litters temporarily—sometimes for several hours—to hunt for food. An absent mother cat may also be busy moving her kittens to a new safe place if she feels the litter may be threatened or at risk in any way. In the process of moving her litter, she may leave a single kitten alone for a short time while she moves another littermate.

On the other hand, don't assume that Mom is coming back, either. You will need to exercise your best judgment in this situation. For example, kittens found in a closed cardboard box have obviously been abandoned by people, and a single tiny kitten discovered in chilly weather will most likely need you to intervene quickly on her behalf. If you're not sure whether or not a litter is abandoned, you'll have to weigh the risks to the kittens. Consider the following: Is the litter located in a relatively safe place? Is the weather warm or cold? Are other animals, traffic, or people threatening the kittens?

If the kittens appear to be safe and comfortable, the general rule of thumb is to wait about eight to ten hours. For whatever reason, a mother cat that does not come for her kittens within that length of time is not able to return to them.

WARMTH FIRST

A mother cat's body heat, not her smell, primarily attracts her newborn kittens. Kittens are unable to see, smell, or hear properly at birth; instead, they sense Mom's

life-giving warmth and clumsily strike out in her direction. Kittens depend on their mother to keep them warm because they cannot maintain their own body temperature—they have only a tiny amount of fat beneath their skin and cannot constrict their skin's blood vessels.

The average (rectal) temperature of a newborn kitten ranges between 92 and 97° F (33 and 36°C). Between 2 and 21 days old, a kitten's temperature will be about 96 to 100°F (35.5 and 38°C).

Experts agree that chilling is the greatest single threat to a neonatal kitten's survival. If a kitten that you find is cold to the touch, hypothermia has already set in. This means that your kitten's body temperature is dangerously low, and her condition is critical. When her body temperature drops, the kitten's blood sugar level also falls below

Your tiny orphan kittens need help fast. This quick overview can direct you to relevant areas of this chapter.

You find a litter of tiny kittens outdoors. Read "What Should I Do First?"

Your kitten is cold. See "Warmth First" and techniques to warm up a chilled kitten.

How soon should I feed my orphan kittens? Read Helpful Hint on stabilizing chilled kittens and "Warmth First."

How can I tell if my kitten is dehydrated? See "Find a Vet."

Should I take the kittens to my veterinarian right away? Refer to "Prevent Dehydration."

What supplies will I need first? Refer to the supplies checklist. The starred items should be acquired first or as soon as possible.

normal, resulting in a hypoglycemic condition. The kitten's internal organs will begin to shut down. At this point, the kitten can lapse into a coma and die.

Abandoned kittens found outside have already lost essential body heat, and this is especially true if the kitten is alone. While you will want to rush to provide lifesaving warmth, keep in mind that warming a kitten too quickly can have an equally terrible effect, resulting in dehydration, shock, or death. A kitten should be warmed slowly

HELPFUL HINT!

Taking a tiny kitten's temperature is a delicate process. Ear thermometers are recommended, but they are expensive. A baby rectal thermometer is often used, but utmost caution should be taken to avoid perforating the kitten's rectum. Ask your veterinarian to show you the correct way to take your kitten's temperature.

over a period of one to three hours, depending on the degree of chilling, until the kitten's body temperature can be maintained above 95°F (35°C).

Try these techniques to warm up a chilled kitten:

• Use your body first. Your own body warmth provides the best immediate insulation, especially if you've just discovered the kittens outside on a cold day. Tuck very young kittens under your outer layer of clothes, such as a coat or fleece vest. (Do not put kittens that display defensive behavior next to your skin or reach for them with bare hands—the kittens may scratch or bite if they are feral.)

• Massage in the warmth. Gently massage the kitten's body to stimulate circulation.

• Wrap a towel around a hot water bottle or bottles of warm water. Place it close to your kitten.

HELPFUL HINT!

Never feed a chilled kitten any type of milk replacement formula. This can prove fatal! To help stabilize a kitten as you warm him, try rubbing .01 cc (a thin layer on your fingertip) of light corn syrup or a tiny amount of honey on his gums, or mix a solution of equal parts sugar and water and give the kitten .01 cc.

BUILD A NEST

As soon as you bring your kittens home, find a quiet place for them in a clean, draft-free area. A sturdy cardboard box or a pet carrier (either should be large enough for the kittens to move around in freely) can provide a comfortable, secure "nest." Thankfully, heating pads designed for pets are now available—be sure to cover the heating pad with a towel and make sure the kitten cannot crawl under it and come in direct contact with the pad. In general, heating pads for people are risky business for orphan kittens. If you must use one, place the heating pad with a protective cover on it down the side and halfway under the box or carrier. Set the temperature on the lowest setting, and cover the bottom of the box with clean towels, cloth diapers, or flannel sheeting. Check the temperature frequently. No matter what type of heating pad you use, make sure it covers only part of the box— orphan kittens must be able to move away from the heat if they become too warm! In addition, a kitten that is too cold to move by herself should not be left on a heating pad. Instead, use bottles of water wrapped in towels to warm the kitten gradually.

Another option is to position an infrared heating light over the kitten's temporary living quarters. Be aware that heat lamps can produce hot spots; to avoid this, set the lamp on low and do not aim it directly over the kittens. Offset it just enough to prevent overheating, and provide a cooler area that the kittens can move to if they become too warm.

While they do need a cooler zone to escape to, ironically, many orphan kittens don't survive because they aren't kept warm enough. This is especially true of a single orphan kitten that doesn't have the benefit of insulating siblings. During his first week of life, a kitten's body temperature is directly related to his environmental temperature. For this reason, the temperature in the kitten area should be 86 to 90°F (30 to 32°C). The temperature can be gradually lowered five degrees a week

A warm nest is crucial in helping your orphan kittens maintain their body heat. *Photo: Isabelle Francais*

The kittens' nest should be kept as clean as possible. Unweaned kittens can generate amazing messes in a short time by relieving themselves in their nest. *Photo: Beverly Adams*

thereafter, until a mild 75°F (24°C) is reached. To regulate the environmental temperature, use a thermometer frequently to check the temperature of the heating pad or other heat source.

SEPARATE FROM OTHER PETS

It's wise to keep your kittens isolated at first. You'll want to protect your vulnerable charges from being stressed or injured by other pets, of course, but there is another important reason as well. Kittens that do not receive their mother's first milk will not have the benefit of colostrum, a protective protein substance that is high in antibodies. These kittens are vulnerable to diseases like feline distemper. A kitten that looks healthy may still harbor a virus. Orphan kittens can also carry parasites such as fleas or worms that can easily pass to other pets with whom they come in contact. Until they receive your veterinarian's okay, confining your orphans helps prevent the spread of any contagious disease or infection to other cats in the household. Wash your hands with antibacterial soap every time you handle your orphans for the same reason.

KEEP IT CLEAN

In addition, you'll want to keep the kitten's environment as clean as possible. Unweaned kittens can generate amazing messes in a short time by relieving themselves in their nest. Steer clear of strong disinfectants and detergents—what's most important is keeping the nest basically clean and dry. Wash any cat-related items, including towels, blankets, and utensils, with 1 part bleach to 12 parts water to cleanse and sterilize them.

PREVENT DEHYDRATION

Dehydration is a condition that involves a considerable loss of water and electrolytes from the body, such as the minerals potassium and sodium. Kittens can easily become dehydrated due to a lack of mother's milk, hypothermia, or prolonged vomiting or diarrhea.

To detect whether a kitten is dehydrated, gently pick up a fold of skin along the kitten's back. The skin should quickly pop back into place. If the skin stays put, dehydration has occurred.

A dehydrated kitten requires quick help. An electrolyte solution made for human babies and sold at most grocery stores is a good first line of defense for mildly dehydrated kittens. You can give your kitten 1 cc of the electrolyte solution (slightly warmed and tested on your wrist) three times a day to help maintain her electrolyte balance.

Severe dehydration is a veterinary emergency. Signs include sunken eyes, lack of skin elasticity as determined by the skin-fold test described above, dry mouth, and extreme exhaustion or lethargy. If your orphan appears to be dehydrated, bring her to a veterinarian immediately. He or she will inject the kitten with a balanced electrolyte solution under the skin or administer a warm nutrient-electrolyte solution by mouth until she responds to the treatment.

FIND A VET

It's important to find a veterinarian who is willing to work with you in a supportive way. Whether or not your kittens look ill, be sure to whisk them off for a health check as soon as possible. The veterinarian will check them for dehydration and other health problems and evaluate their general condition. The kittens will also be checked for worms and parasites. Most important, your veterinarian can help provide the basic supplies you'll need, along with helpful advice and information.

KEEP GOOD RECORDS

While keeping thorough records won't be your very first concern, it ranks right up there as one of the most important aspects of caring for orphan kittens, according to Alley Cat Allies, a national feral cat network. The organization recommends charting the kitten's initial weight, taking notes on the kitten's general appearance, and accurately recording the feeding schedule with the time and amount of formula dispensed. Examples of a weight chart, feeding schedule, and progress chart are provided in the Appendix at the end of this book.

Initially, it may be difficult to find time to make detailed notes. Do the best you can. Keep in mind that the information you gather on each kitten now may help you make informed decisions regarding a kitten's health care later. Plus, your veterinarian will bless you.

Anything you can do for kittens, a mother cat can do better. Finding a mother cat to foster your orphan kittens provides their best chance of survival. *Photo: Jacquie DeLillo*

Fostering Kittens

Anything you can do for kittens, a mother cat can do better. Before you take on the time-consuming job of hand-feeding kittens yourself, it is worthwhile to try to find a healthy feline foster mother. She can provide your orphans with their best chance for survival. Most mother cats are willing to accept needy kittens that aren't their own and allow them to nurse. Besides the obvious benefits of an abundant supply of mother's milk, a feline foster mom can also provide a more natural environment for the kittens during their first critical weeks of life. But where can you find a mother cat? Consider these options:

Call an animal shelter. Explain your situation and ask shelter staff whether they are housing any female cats that are raising litters. Many shelters have members or volunteers who care for orphan kittens, and they may be able to offer help or advice. Do not, however, drop the kittens off at your local shelter and assume that

A shelter, veterinarian, breeder, or cat rescue group may be able to help you locate a suitable foster mother for your orphans.
Photo: Isabelle Francais

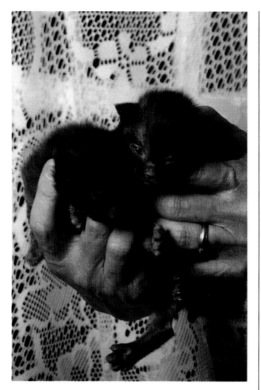

To introduce your orphans to the mother cat, rub all of the kittens together to establish the scent of the "old" kittens onto the "new" ones.
Photo: Isabelle Francais

Under most circumstances, the foster mother will quickly adopt the new kittens, and soon you won't be able to tell which litter is which.
Photo: Beverly Adams

staff members will raise them until they are adoptable. Before taking orphan kittens to a shelter, it's important to find out what services it provides. While the number of shelters with foster pet programs is growing, the reality is that many have limited resources and are not equipped to supply the intensive care required for unweaned kittens. Unfortunately, shelters receiving litters of tiny kittens often are forced to euthanize them.

Ask your veterinarian. He or she may be able to help or refer you to someone who can provide assistance.

Talk to cat rescue groups, breeders, and cat clubs in your area. This may take some homework on your part, but many members of such groups are willing to offer help or suggestions.

HANDLING INTRODUCTIONS

If you are lucky enough to find a healthy foster queen who is current on vaccinations and at the right stage of lactation, introduce your kittens to her as soon as possible. The kittens should be younger than four weeks old (older kittens can be weaned). To protect the health of the mother cat, introduce her only to healthy kittens that have been checked by a veterinarian. Sickly kittens should not be placed with a foster queen.

One experienced shelter manager's recipe for successfully introducing orphan kittens to a foster queen involves placing the scent of the feline mom's kittens on each orphan kitten. To try this method, take one kitten from the queen and one orphan kitten and put them together in your hands. Gently but thoroughly rub and roll the kittens together to establish the scent of the "old" kittens onto the "new" kittens.

The foster mom will usually adopt the needy kittens quickly. Quietly observe the litter for an hour; you'll be able to tell within a short time whether the foster mom will welcome the new kittens. A willing queen will show acceptance by licking and cleaning the new kittens; she will then lie down and allow the kittens to nurse.

It's a good idea to decide on an age for weaning the kittens and arrange a date to take them home. Until the kittens are adoptable, you should continue to be responsible for their welfare.

YOU CAN DO IT

If you are unable to find a feline foster mom, do not despair. With a little knowledge and lots of nurturing, you can guide your kittens through their first fragile weeks and tilt the odds in their favor. You should, however, know a few things before you start. Parenting orphan kittens is hard work. It will take your time, commitment, and nearly all the energy you can muster for at least a few weeks. As one humane organization put it, a kitten is a baby and requires the same special care and attention that every baby needs.

As you begin caring for your orphan kittens, consider that warmth, acceptance, and consistency—the same parental qualities that can produce a healthy child—can lead to a healthy kitten, as Deborah Rumberger stated in a *Cat Fancy* magazine article several years ago. I never tire of passing her quote along, because her advice rings so true. Keep it in mind as you care for your kitten's basic needs.

No matter how hard you try to be a surrogate mom for your kittens, however, it's important to realize that you may not always succeed in bringing them to adulthood. It may help you to know that kittens born under the best of circumstances do not always survive. If your kittens have severe health problems or appear to be fighting a painful downhill battle, your veterinarian can help you make the difficult decision to continue

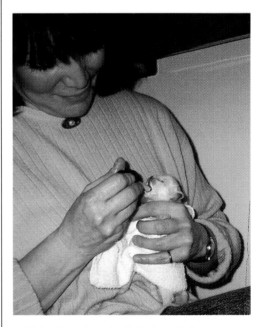

With hard work and a little knowledge, you can raise your fragile orphans yourself.
Photo: Jacquie DeLillo

To raise your kittens successfully, remember that a kitten is a baby and requires the same care and attention that every baby needs. *Photo: John Tyson*

THE GUIDE TO HANDRAISING KITTENS

treating them or to end their suffering through euthanasia. The need for working with a supportive veterinarian cannot be stressed enough. He or she can diagnose medical problems, illness, or physical defects that may or may not be preventable and/or cured. More than any other person, the right veterinarian will understand the feelings and emotions you experience and will help you work through them. Many pet loss support groups also now exist through veterinary colleges and on the Internet. Sharing your

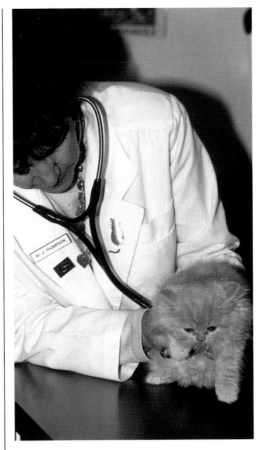

Your orphans should receive a veterinary checkup as soon as possible, even if they appear to be healthy. *Photo: Joan Balzarini*

loss with others can help reduce the grief you encounter.

Orphan kittens already have a strike or two against them—they may be malnourished, chilled, or ill before you find them. Their immune systems are likely to be weakened, and they may not have received the protective first milk their mother would normally provide. Despite these factors, many orphan kittens exhibit a strong desire to live by relentlessly crying for food. They will fight to survive, and with your help they may thrive—if the foster parent takes the time to do things right and gets capable veterinary care along the way.

YOUR KITTEN'S FIRST VETERINARY APPOINTMENT

Your orphans should receive a veterinary checkup as soon as possible, even if they appear to be the picture of health. Your veterinarian will give each kitten a full physical exam from nose to tail—including listening to the heart and lungs, feeling the abdominal cavity, and checking physical development. In addition, your kitten will be checked for worms and other parasites and may be tested for feline leukemia, a fatal virus that kittens acquire from their mother or other cats.

Your veterinarian will set up a vaccination schedule adapted to your individual kitten and her environment, but you can generally expect the following first vaccines, based on the vaccine protocol of the American Association of Feline Practitioners and the Academy of Feline Medicine: Feline rhinotracheitis–panleukopenia–calicivirus #1. A rabies vaccine won't be given until your kitten reaches at least 12 weeks of age, when your kitten receives her second feline rhinotracheitis vaccination. All other vaccines, such as the feline leukemia, chlamydia, and feline infectious peritonitis vaccines, are considered optional, depending on risk factors, efficacy, and safety.

Hand-Feeding Kittens

Feeding orphan kittens doesn't have to be complicated or confusing, but it does require that you follow a few important guidelines and use some good old common sense. For example, kittens need impressive amounts of nutrients and energy for healthy growth. Their energy level requirements dictate how much food they should receive. Computing the daily amount of formula to feed down to the kilocalorie, however, isn't necessary. You can refer to the feeding chart in this chapter to determine your kitten's daily nutritional needs.

Healthy kittens gain weight rapidly after birth, usually doubling their weight after one week. They continue to gain

HELPFUL HINT!

To safely weigh tiny kittens at home, use a kitchen baking scale that contains a large capacity bowl. For example, one baking scale comes with an extra-large bowl that allows you to figure weight amounts to nearly seven pounds.

This eight-hour-old kitten, named Veritas, is less than six inches long and virtually helpless.
Photo: Jacquie DeLillo

Age (Days)	Weight
1	2 $\frac{1}{2}$ to 4 $\frac{3}{4}$ ounces
5	3 to 7 ounces
10	4 $\frac{1}{2}$ to 9 $\frac{3}{4}$ ounces
15	6 to 11 $\frac{3}{4}$ ounces
20	7 $\frac{1}{2}$ to 14 $\frac{1}{2}$ ounces
25	8 to 16 $\frac{3}{4}$ ounces

Reprinted courtesy of Alley Cat Allies

approximately half an ounce each day. A kitten that loses weight should be closely monitored by a veterinarian. Like all individuals, kitten weights vary. The average weight chart can help you determine the normal weight ranges for your kittens. You will want to weigh your kittens regularly to make sure they are growing properly, but chances are you will be able to tell whether your kittens are thriving or not. A healthy kitten grows at an extraordinary rate, and her body, bones, and organs will continue to develop until she is a year old.

Orphan kittens may not grow at the same pace as those that have the benefits of their natural mom; even so, understanding the normal early development of healthy kittens can help you figure out where your orphans stand.

HELPFUL HINT!

If the kitten's eyes don't open or seem crusted over, try gently cleaning them with cotton balls dipped in warm water.

At six days old, Veritas is able to crawl, although he is still blind and nearly deaf.
Photo: Jacquie DeLillo

STAGES OF EARLY GROWTH
First Week
Kittens are virtually helpless at birth. Tiny and wet, they generally weigh in between three and four ounces and are less than six inches long. The kitten's eyes are closed and her ears are folded over—at birth she is both blind and deaf. During the first week, her sense of smell, hearing, and taste begin to take shape. She can't walk yet, but she is born with a rooting reflex. She cannot urinate or defecate on her own either, but she has the ability to make pint-sized distress calls and to purr. Newborns spend 90 percent of their time sleeping; the other 10 percent of the time they are busy nursing.

Second Week
The kitten's eyes begin to open (they are blue) and focus a little bit. The ears also begin to open and stand up. She moves

At 12 days old, Veritas' eyes are open and he is able to walk a little. His ears are also beginning to open. *Photo: Jacquie DeLillo*

around, begins to crawl, and snuggles in her nest. She cannot yet retract her tiny claws, but kneads enthusiastically.

Third Week

The kitten's eyesight improves. Those important first steps take place in the form of wobbly movements. She starts to cut baby teeth and takes frequent tumbles. True eye color appears. She begins to notice the world around her—full of sights, sounds, and siblings.

Fourth Week

Four-week-old kittens are busy exploring their environment, playing with littermates, and learning how to dig. They roll over and get back up. They begin lapping and can go to the bathroom without help. Litter box training begins.

Fifth Week

Vigorous kitten play, including hiding, stalking, and pouncing, is the norm by the fifth week. Baby teeth are in. Individual personalities emerge. The process of weaning and learning to nibble solid food continues.

Sixth Week and Beyond

By the sixth week, the kitten's balancing act has improved, thanks to the wise use of her tail as a steering mechanism. She learns to negotiate her territory, trotting and running in a smoother fashion. She is more

The two-and-a-half-week-old Veritas has improved eyesight and has begun to notice the world around him. *Photo: Jacquie DeLillo*

At three weeks old, Veritas takes frequent tumbles, but his motor skills are developing rapidly. *Photo: Jacquie DeLillo*

Vigorous kitten play is the rule at four-and-a-half weeks old. Litter box training and weaning has also begun. *Photo: Jacquie DeLillo*

playful, begins to use her nails to climb, and thrives on physical and mental stimulation.

COLOSTRUM

The first milk that a kitten receives from her mother is rich in protein and nutrients, containing antibodies that help protect kittens from disease until they are weaned. Kittens absorb colostrum through the intestines for a few days after birth. The level of protection the kitten receives depends on the antibody level in the mother cat's blood. A kitten that does not receive colostrum will be extremely vulnerable to disease and, if possible, should receive vaccinations early. (Kittens

GIRL OR BOY?

To determine the sex of your kittens, gently lift their tails, take a peek, and keep English punctuation in mind. The anus, testes, and penis will resemble an exclamation point on males. Females will exhibit an anus and vulva that looks remarkably like a colon.

normally receive their first vaccinations at eight weeks of age.) Consult your veterinarian to determine the best time to vaccinate your kittens.

FEED ME

Movies and books often depict hungry kittens enthusiastically lapping up saucers of cow's milk, but don't jump on this bandwagon. Cow's milk should never be given to orphan kittens. It's a poor substitute for a mother cat's milk—for example, the lactose level in cow's milk is too high and the fat level and protein too low for kittens. Even worse, cow's milk often causes diarrhea, which can quickly dehydrate your orphans.

Instead, look for premixed formulas that approximate a feline mother's milk. Milk replacer formulas are available in liquid or

Quite grown up in appearance at 17 weeks, Veritas is still a kitten at heart. *Photo: Jacquie DeLillo*

GENERAL FEEDING CHART

Kitten's Age (Weeks)	Average Weight	Amount of Formula Per Day (cubic cm.)	Number of Feedings Daily
1	4 oz.	32 cc	6
2	7 oz.	56 cc	4
3	10 oz.	80 cc	3
4	13 oz.	104 cc	3
5	1 lb.	128 cc	3

powdered form. Liquid, ready-to-use formulas are more convenient—you just warm them up and serve—but the powdered variety has a longer shelf life and is more reasonably priced, especially if you are caring for a large litter. (Follow the manufacturer's directions on the label for proper preparation, administration, and storage.) Both formula types, along with nursing bottles to feed them with, can be purchased at pet supply stores and veterinary clinics.

Homemade formulas for kittens are also popular, but it's essential to run any homemade recipe past your veterinarian before trying one. Commercially prepared formulas are generally preferred for their closer composition to feline mother's milk.

New foster parents are often surprised to discover how frequently very small kittens should be fed—as much as every other hour or more around the clock at first! Neonatal kittens have tiny tummies and only a minute amount of fat under the skin, so kittens younger than three weeks of age should receive small feedings often. Frequent meals also help prevent the

kitten's kidneys and digestive system from overloading.

It's important not to overfeed or underfeed your kitten. Overfeeding can cause serious health problems that begin with diarrhea and end with dehydration. One way to tell whether you're consistently feeding too much is the appearance of a grayish stool. On the other hand, a kitten that is not fed enough will cry continuously and appear restless, then listless. Underfeeding will result in the kitten becoming dehydrated and chilled.

What to do? Here's where common sense can help. Keep in mind that a kitten's milk intake is limited by her small stomach. Her stomach should feel full but not swollen after she is fed. Apply this general rule of thumb: A kitten requires about 8 cc's of formula per ounce of body weight a day, divided among feedings. Follow the general feeding guide provided, but realize that each kitten is an individual and feeding is not an exact science. Healthy kittens let you know when they want to be fed and will often let you know they are full by releasing the nipple. If your kitten wakes up

Milk replacers for kittens are available in liquid or powdered form. The powdered variety has a longer shelf life and is less expensive. *Photo: Weems Hutto*

You can hand-feed kittens using several different devices, including (from left) a syringe, a standard small-animal bottle, an eyedropper, and a more elaborate small-animal bottle. *Photo: Weems Hutto*

One bottle brand that garners high marks from foster parents is distinctive for its wide-angled shape and long, thin, pliable nipples. *Photo: Weems Hutto*

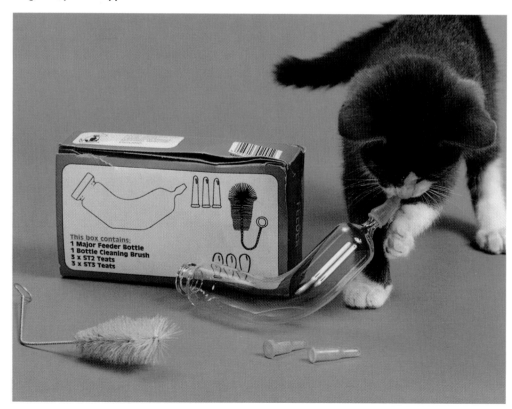

Many kitten caretakers swear by their own homemade kitten formulas, but it's a good idea to check with your veterinarian before using one. This homemade formula has been successfully tested on kittens by veterinarians.

> One 12-ounce can of evaporated skim milk
> One 4-ounce can of evaporated whole cow's milk
> 4 ounces of plain yogurt
> Three egg yolks

Mix all ingredients well and strain. Serve slightly warmer than room temperature. Before serving, test a few drops on your wrist to make sure the formula is comfortably warm. Keep unused formula refrigerated at all times. Store for up to four days, and always check to make sure the formula is still fresh.

Reprinted with permission from the Homeless Cat Network

and cries, she is probably hungry. On the other hand, don't wake a well-fed kitten that sleeps past her two-hour feeding. Observe your kitten and adjust her feeding schedule accordingly.

FEEDING METHODS

You can hand-feed kittens in one of three ways—by using a bottle made for that purpose, an eyedropper, or a tube. Massage your kitten gently before feeding her to provide a little exercise and to help stimulate her muscles and circulation.

Bottle-Feeding

Kittens that are strong enough to suck vigorously on your finger should be bottle-fed. Nursing bottles for kittens are sold at most pet supply stores and veterinary clinics. You can also purchase them from pet-related Web sites or directly from companies that produce them.

One popular brand, identified by its bright blue logo, is inexpensive and easy to find. A variety of nursing kits are available from this company, including a starter emergency feeding kit specifically designed for orphan kittens. This kit includes a two-ounce reusable nurser bottle and nipple, powdered kitten milk replacer, and a small amount of a palatable gel that contains beneficial bacteria to help relieve intestinal distress.

Another bottle brand that garners high marks from foster parents is a little more difficult to locate but is distinctive for its wide-angled shape and long, thin, pliable nipples. The standard feeding package includes a bottle, three nipples in two sizes, and a bottle cleaning brush.

Depending which brand you choose, you may need to place (or enlarge) the hole in the nipple yourself. To do this, use a hot needle or pin to poke a small hole in the nipple's top or make a small cross-cut with a razor blade or very sharp scissors. Important: Enlarge the hole just enough to allow the formula to drip slowly from the nipple when the bottle is inverted.

Be sure to sterilize all utensils before each feeding and warm the formula to no more than 100°F (38°C). Test the formula on your wrist—it should feel warm, not hot, on your skin. Make sure the formula contains no hot spots if you use a microwave oven to warm it.

To bottle-feed a kitten, visualize the kitten's natural position if she were nursing from her mother. Place your kitten stomach-down on a towel she can cling to at roughly a 45-degree angle. Squeeze a drop of milk on the tip of the nipple, gently open her mouth, and slip the nipple between her jaws. The angle helps prevent air from entering the stomach, and a slight tension on the bottle encourages sucking.

Never hold the kitten in the air or on her back while you feed her. Keep your kitten from slipping with one hand while holding the bottle with the other. Hold the bottle so your kitten does not ingest air, and never force-feed your kitten or squeeze the bottle to force the last of the formula out. Instead, let the kitten suck the formula at her own pace. Then relax. You and your kitten will quickly catch on.

When your kitten is full, her tummy will be slightly rounded and bubbles will form around her mouth. Just like young human babies, kittens must be burped after each feeding. Burp your kitten by holding her

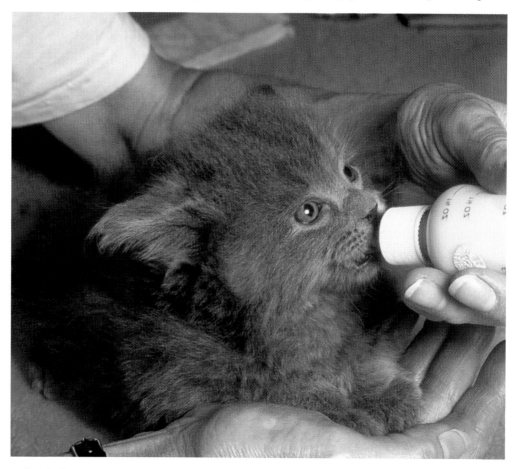

To bottle-feed a kitten, place the kitten in her natural nursing position, stomach-down at a 45-degree angle. *Photo: John Tyson*

upright against your shoulder. Pat and rub her gently on her back.

Eyedropper

Feeding a kitten with a sterilized eyedropper is more time-consuming than bottle-feeding and often less accurate. It's considered a less desirable way to feed kittens, but an eyedropper can serve as a temporary nurser until a bottle is obtained. Eyedroppers may also benefit very young kittens that begin drinking formula a few drops at a time. When they start to draw the formula out themselves, the kittens can be switched to a bottle. Follow the same guidelines that you would for bottle-feeding. Squeeze the formula from the eyedropper slowly to avoid forcing fluid into the kitten's lungs.

Tube-Feeding

This method is recommended for weak or ill kittens that are unable to suckle or

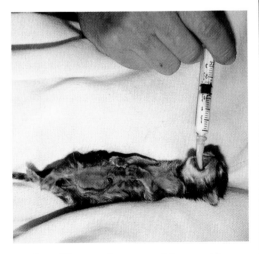

Weak or ill kittens that are unable to suckle may be tube-fed, as shown here. Consult your veterinarian for hands-on training and the proper equipment before attempting this techinque. *Photo: Ginger S. Buck*

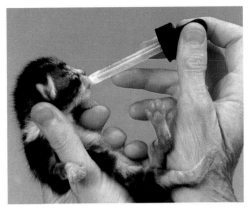

Eyedroppers are a good way to feed very young kittens that begin drinking formula a few drops at a time. *Photo: Weems Hutto*

that refuse bottle-feeding. Tube-feeding is a fast, efficient way to feed orphan kittens, but it must be done carefully to avoid passing fluid into the lungs, a dangerous condition that can quickly lead to pneumonia and death. Foster parents can learn how to skillfully administer tube-feedings fairly easily, but the procedure should not be learned from a book. Consult your veterinarian or other knowledgeable caretaker for hands-on training and the proper equipment.

The tube-feeding method works by using an appropriately sized infant feeding tube (for instance, a number 5 French is used for kittens weighing less than 10 ounces) or small soft rubber catheter and a syringe to inject commercially prepared formula directly into the stomach. The distance from the kitten's last rib to the tip of her nose must be carefully measured and marked off on the feeding tube (a piece of tape works well, as does a marker). Measure the tube length frequently to adjust for the kitten's rapid growth. Weigh her and give the correct amount of formula (warmed to

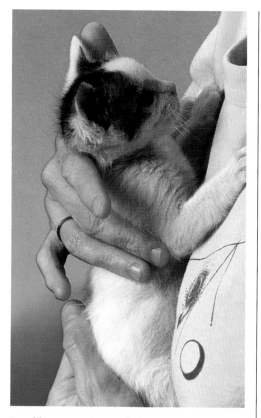

Just like young human babies, kittens must be burped after each feeding. Hold the kitten upright against your shoulder and rub her back gently. *Photo: Weems Hutto*

If your kitten appears to choke during a feeding, or you notice formula coming out of his nose, don't panic. The kitten may have aspirated some of the formula into his lungs. Immediately and gently hold the kitten upside down until the choking or coughing subsides. Tip: Make sure the hole in the kitten's nursing bottle nipple is not too large!

Watch for the following problems:

• If your kitten begins to choke, remove the feeding tube until she has recovered.

• Remove the tube if you feel resistance before reaching the tape mark—the tube may be in the kitten's trachea.

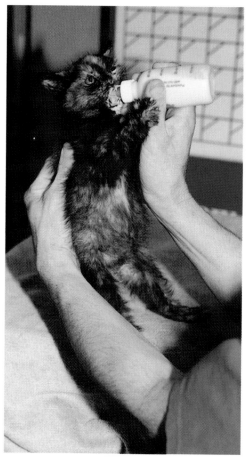

Never hold the kitten in the air or on her back while you feed her. *Photo: Ginger S. Buck*

approximately 100° F [38° C]) to avoid overfeeding and regurgitation. After filling, connect the tube to the syringe. Make sure that any air in the tube or syringe is expelled by pointing the syringe up to the ceiling and pushing out any air that may be inside. To tube-feed, the kitten's head should be held in the normal nursing posture, the mouth open slightly, and the moistened feeding tube gently passed over her tongue and into the throat until you reach the tape mark on the feeding tube. Never force the tube into the kitten. Once in place, the formula-filled syringe should be emptied very slowly over a two-minute period to prevent the fluid from passing into the lungs.

• If regurgitation occurs, remove the feeding tube and wait until the next scheduled meal to tube-feed your kitten.

• Tube-fed kittens do not get the chance to suckle normally, which sometimes results in misplaced suckling on other kittens. You may have to separate the offending kitten from the others if this occurs.

STIMULATION MEANS ELIMINATION

Kittens younger than three weeks of age cannot eliminate by themselves—they need your help. A mother cat normally licks the kittens' genital and anal areas to stimulate them to urinate and defecate. You can teach your orphan kitten these vital basics by following this procedure: After feeding and burping your kitten, take a cotton ball moistened with warm water and gently rub over the kitten's stomach and bottom. This action mimics a mother cat's licking and stimulates the kitten to relieve themselves. (You may get the same response by running a damp forefinger along the kitten's abdominal wall.) You will need to do this after every meal until your kittens can eliminate on their own.

WASH AFTER EVERY MEAL

Tiny kittens are irresistibly cute, but they are also notoriously messy and sticky babies. Like a mother cat, you'll want to clean them up after meals or after they eliminate. Don't immerse a kitten in water, which can cause respiratory problems. Instead, wash her with a warm, damp washcloth. Use short, gentle strokes to imitate a mother cat cleaning her kittens with licks of her tongue. Towel-dry gently. For very wet kittens, use a blow dryer on the lowest setting and from a safe distance. Never allow your kittens to become chilled.

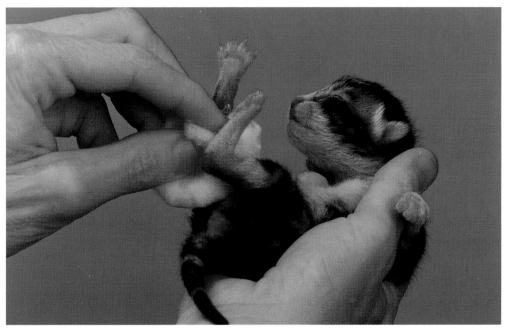

After feeding and burping the kitten, lightly touching the genital area with a moistened cotton ball will stimulate her to eliminate. *Photo: Weems Hutto*

Weaning Your Kitten

The first thing to learn about weaning is that kittens, being the wonderful species and individuals that they are, do not always stick to the schedule we plan for them. That is, weaning has a lot more to do with a kitten's readiness to be weaned than our desire to hurry the process along. When a

Convincing a kitten to give up a yummy bottle for solid food may prove difficult, but it will happen.
Photo: Ginger S. Buck

mother cat raises her kittens, weaning depends on the kitten's desire to continue nursing and the queen's cooperation (or lack thereof) in furnishing this all-hours service. For example, weaning may occur earlier for a feral kitten that needs to learn how to hunt to eat than for the indoor kitten that can't quite understand why she has to give up warm mother's milk for dry kitten food.

As a foster parent, you may be anxious to wean your kittens as soon as possible. It's understandable. After all, sleeping through the night and resuming a normal life may seem tantalizingly just out of reach. My advice? Be patient. With a little encouragement, your kittens will graduate to solid food quickly.

ON YOUR MARK
When your kittens reach the four-week mark—occasionally earlier—you can begin the weaning process. Start by putting the formula in a shallow bowl or pan. (An

Start the weaning process by putting formula in a shallow bowl, and begin to add solid canned food gradually. *Photo: Isabelle Francais*

experienced shelter manager I know successfully uses Frisbees® instead of pans. They are just the right height and are easily cleaned, she says.) Neatness doesn't count right now—be prepared for some wildly messy moments as your "preschoolers" learn to eat from a pan and not in it. At the same time, start leaving out fresh water (filtered or spring water is best) in shallow dishes. From this point on, fresh water should be available at all times.

Continue to keep your kittens as clean and dry as possible. Like a mother cat, you will teach your kittens to clean their fur and groom themselves. The old adage about cleanliness being next to godliness—a cliché that cats surely invented—can also prevent a host of skin problems from developing.

Begin to add solid food gradually. Your approach may vary at this point, but I recommend introducing a high-quality canned food designed specifically for growing kittens. Offer a mix of two parts canned food blended with one part formula. Encourage your kitten to eat the mixture by

When the kittens are eating only canned food and water, it's time to add dry food.
Photo: Vincent Serbin

smearing some on the kitten's lips, or touch a finger to the mixture and then put it into your kitten's mouth.

One experienced caretaker who has successfully raised hundreds of orphan kittens gradually adds moist kitten food to the formula until they eat only the moist food. At this time, a high-quality dry kitten food is made available to the kittens. Once the kittens aim for the dry food, they are slowly switched over.

You can reduce your kitten's bottle-feeding when she starts to eat more frequently from her pan. This is where you may run into a bit of a hold-up, because your kitten may not be as excited about dry kibble as you are. Be patient at this point and realize that it takes time for young kittens to become strong enough to chew dry kitten food. Weaning should not be

Your kitten may not be as excited about dry kibble as you are, but by six weeks of age, weaning should be complete. *Photo: Isabelle Francais*

finished until your kittens are six weeks of age or older.

Your kitten will probably eat about three solid meals daily as she continues to drink formula. Pay close attention to stools during the weaning process, because changes in diet can often cause diarrhea.

Gradually reduce the amount of liquid in the mix until your kitten eats only solid food.

Feed your kittens all the food they can consume. Growing kittens rarely overeat. Studies show that kittens fed unlimited amounts of food will eat every few hours or nibble at it frequently, regardless of the type of food (dry or canned) available. Experts recommend free-choice feeding or feeding at least three times a day during a kitten's growth. It's also wise to

KITTEN FEEDING DO'S AND DON'TS

Do
Do keep your kitten's water dish filled at all times.
Do feed your kitten food that contains consistently high-quality ingredients for kittens.
Do put out only what your kitten will eat in 24 hours.
Do replace food that has been moistened or mixed with canned food every 24 hours.

Don't
Don't feed your kitten cow's milk—she cannot digest it easily.
Don't feed your kitten food that contains onion—it can cause anemia.
Don't feed your kitten regular canned tuna—it can cause vitamin E deficiency.

Reprinted courtesy of IAMS Company

expose your kittens to a variety of food types and flavors, because cats learn taste preference by six months of age.

READY, SET, GO!

Hurray! Your kitten is now ready for a litter box. Her first litter box should allow for easy access—a small litter box or a pie tin with a shallow layer of litter works well. Your kitten will be attracted to the movable texture of the litter. She may begin the process of "earth-raking," or moving the litter around with her front paws, a behavior kittens exhibit shortly before they begin eliminating in the litter box. Don't be surprised if you notice a small amount of litter around the kitten's mouth at this time.

Place the litter pan within reach of the kitten, and after meals, place your kitten gently in the litter pan. You can interest her by scratching the litter yourself, but chances are she will quickly figure out what to do all by herself. Covering or burying waste, however, is taught by the queen, so you may want to show your orphan kitten how to do this. It's also a good idea to keep the litter box close to the kitten's center of activity for a while; like small children, kittens need to relieve themselves as soon as they recognize the urge to go. You can move the litter box to a less conspicuous place as your kitten grows up.

HELPFUL HINT!

Start your kitten out with clay litter—not clumping litter—for safety's sake. Fine clumping litter can stick to kittens that are still drinking formula and is tough to remove.

Introduce a litter box at about the same time as you begin to introduce solid food. Most kittens will figure out what it is for on their own. *Photo: Beverly Adams*

Sense and Sociability

Kittens need to be touched. Touch, whether a mother cat's or a human's, is not only calming, healing, and pleasurable to a kitten, it's critical for his healthy emotional development. Many touchable, tangible things happen when kittens are raised in

litters with a mother cat. They constantly bump, push, and even step on (and over) their siblings and Mom.

This doesn't mean you should ever treat your orphans roughly, nor should you allow anyone else to do so. Never pick up a kitten by the scruff of his neck or by his legs, for example, and supervise small children around the kittens. Kids and kittens can go well together—both love to play and cuddle—if children learn to respect the kittens' needs. Ask children to sit back and let the kittens get used to them; then teach youngsters how to handle the kittens gently to avoid injuring them.

PROVEN TOUCH

Touch, gentle and nurturing, stimulates the development of neural pathways in young kittens and helps build strong bonds with the people in their lives. Research shows that kittens that are not touched by a human being until seven weeks of age are less responsive to people in general. In addition,

Kids and kittens can go well together. Both love to play and cuddle. *Photo: Wendy Nelson*

kittens older than seven weeks that do not come in contact with other animals are often unable to develop social bonds with them, viewing them instead as something to flee from or eat. One well-known writer describes this early time as a magic window opening in a blossoming kitten's psychological development. Use this time, which lasts roughly three months, to lay a solid foundation for your orphan kittens so that they may become outgoing and confident adult cats.

SOCIALIZE, SOCIALIZE

Start by establishing a social life for your cats. All kittens need a social life, of course, but socialization is even more vital for orphan kittens. Because they are deprived of the natural mother's input to contribute to their temperaments, you will need to take over the task. Begin by getting down on their level, literally, and quietly and gently handle your kittens for short periods of time, about 10 to 15 minutes. This will come pretty naturally as you care for them. One veterinarian recommends this method of first gentle handling: Pick the kittens up daily, turn them over on their backs, and gently stroke their tummies. The kittens will not only get used to being handled, but you will have the opportunity to check their health. Be on the lookout for external parasites like fleas, as well as any odors that may signify a health problem. Slowly increase the amount of time you spend with them.

This is a good time to really get to know the emerging personalities of your kittens. All cats, like people, are individuals. Spend time observing your kittens, as well as interacting with them. While it may seem contradictory, also be careful not to handle them too much. For example, don't disturb

Normal kittens constantly bump, push, and even step on their siblings. Touch is very important to the kittens' emotional development. *Photo: Beverly Adams*

THE GUIDE TO HANDRAISING KITTENS

It is important to handle your kittens gently and frequently so that they get used to a human's touch.
Photo: Ginger S. Buck

sleeping kittens, and respect a kitten's wish to be put down when she thinks she has been carried for too long. Don't stare directly into your kittens' eyes—kittens and cats regard this as rude, challenging behavior. Learning to appreciate the needs and limits of your individual kittens will help you balance the interaction that comes naturally to mother cats.

As the kittens develop, safely expose them to a variety of normal household sounds and animals. Introduce them to family members, friends, and people of all ages and sizes. One longtime foster mom I know likes to take her weaned kittens on short car rides in their pet carriers—an experience that often terrifies adult cats. (Note: She never leaves them alone in the car.) The experience helps her kittens adjust to new situations and reduces stress during trips to the veterinarian.

HELPFUL HINT!

To pick your kitten up in a way that makes her feel safe and secure, put one hand under her back legs and the other around her chest.

Special Needs of Single Kittens

Under ordinary circumstances, a kitten's littermates offer each other round-the-clock comfort, warmth, security and, when they are older, playtime. Single kittens don't have these options, of course, but there are several things you can do to make them feel less lonely and a lot more comfortable and secure.

PROVIDE WARMTH

Without her mother's body warmth and the secondary heat that a pile of brothers and sisters generate, a single newborn kitten cannot maintain a normal body temperature. Keeping your kitten warm enough is your first priority, so be sure to follow the guidelines outlined in the section on first aid.

Single kittens don't have the round-the-clock comfort, warmth, security, and playtime of kittens with littermates. *Photo: Weems Hutto*

A single newborn kitten may have trouble maintaining a normal body temperature. Keeping your single kitten warm enough should be your first priority. *Photo: Wendy Nelson*

Place a stuffed animal nearby so an "only" kitten has something furry to climb over and around or just to snuggle by. *Photo: Robert Pearcy*

KEEP HER COMPANY

Neonatal kittens do not normally lie quietly alone for long periods of time. Life is active in a nest with several kittens—full of licking, bumping, crawling, pushing, purring, crying, and soft breathing. All this action helps promote normal development, healthy exercise, and socialization, which is why you should never leave a single kitten alone for hours without any stimulating or tactile experiences. Instead, hold and touch your single kitten often. Let her rest against the warmth of your skin. Indulge her instinctive need to suckle by offering a soft cloth or your finger.

Props

Place a stuffed animal nearby so an "only" kitten has something furry to climb over and around or just to snuggle by. The substitute sibling should be safe and washable. It should not contain string, buttons, or any other small parts that a

A stuffed animal with something special packed inside may be the most comforting product ever developed for single orphan kittens. One new product is a stuffed animal that contains a heat pack and a plastic heart with a battery-operated "heartbeat." The product simulates body warmth and the rhythmic sounds of a heart, and foster parents report that orphan kittens approach, climb over, and even knead the tummy of the stuffed surrogate mom just as they would a real mother cat.

These special stuffed animals contain no small parts that can be chewed; the eyes and other facial features are stitched on with thread. Velcro® seals the belly pocket containing the nontoxic heat source—a heat pack made from natural materials that stays warm for up to 20 hours. Cat owners can alternatively place dry rice into a terry-cloth pouch that also comes with the product. The rice can be heated quickly in a microwave oven and stays warm in the pouch for up to three hours.

The product is machine washable, but the best part is that it feels and sounds like a real mother cat—good news for "only" kittens.

kitten might ingest. Animal shapes made of imitation lambswool that are sold specifically for pets are a safe option. A ticking clock hidden safely under towels or within a stuffed animal can also provide some comfort and reassurance in the nest.

SOCIALIZE HER

Because their mother isn't around to teach them about life, single kittens particularly need to learn how to interact with other cats (and other people) socially, in a positive way. It's been proven that kittens older than seven weeks that do not interact with other animals have trouble creating social bonds with them. A kitten raised only by a human may become antisocial in her relations with other cats and possibly with other people as well. If your kitten is healthy, she should be introduced to other friendly adult cats and people to boost her social development.

Don't stop there, though. Annie Bruce, author of *Cat Be Good* and a cat owner consultant in Boulder, Colorado, offers the following creative tips for socializing your only kitten. Perhaps she will inspire you to come up with a few ideas of your own.

Use Your Hands

Hold and pet your kitten 20 minutes or more each day. Touch your kitten often to give her as much human contact as possible.

Massage Her Feet

Gently massage your kitten's feet every day to get her used to having her nails trimmed later. When your kitten is about three weeks old, begin trimming a tiny amount off one or two nails each day.

Do Housework Together

Figure out a way to carry your kitten safely in a frontal sling and do housework together. (One company offers a sling just for that purpose, which looks similar to a human baby carrier and attaches in front.) Your kitten will enjoy the interaction and the sound of your heartbeat.

Show Her Noise Is Normal

Music and noise help socialize kittens. Subjecting kittens to reasonable amounts of noise can prevent them from turning into "fraidy-cats" later. Periods of quiet time are fine, but expose your kitten to a variety of noises daily. Let her listen to cartoons, a radio, or even your husband's blues band, along with all the usual household noises. Act like noise, sometimes even a loud noise, is a perfectly normal event.

One product that's specially made to comfort orphan kittens is a stuffed animal that contains a heat pack and a plastic heart with a battery-operated heartbeat. *Photo: Weems Hutto*

Express Yourself

Talk, or better yet sing, your kitten's praises frequently to get her used to the sound of human voices.

Ask Kids to Help

The most laid-back kittens are often those fostered in homes with children. If you don't have kids, ask a child in your neighborhood to visit your kitten. Children love to handle kittens, and kittens can learn to appreciate them if the children are taught to respect the kittens' needs and limits. Be sure to supervise their interaction.

Share the Steam

Put your kitten in the bathroom while you take a bath or shower. The steam is good for both of you, and your kitten will get used to the sound of water. Treat your kitten to a massage during her steamy encounter.

Provide a Scratching Post

Encourage your kitten to climb her scratching post as early as she is able to, or about four weeks old. This will build muscles and confidence.

Teach a Few No-No's

Reserve your hands for massage, petting, and treats. Never allow your hands or ankles to be used as play toys; use a real toy instead. Do not allow or encourage a kitten to bite or climb up your leg, even when she is very young. Keep lots of cat toys handy to redirect a kitten that wants to "attack" you in play.

Scheduling "play dates" with other healthy kittens will help your single kitten to adjust to life with other people and animals. *Photo: Weems Hutto*

Toys and a cozy scratching post will help teach your single kitten that hands, feet, and furniture are not acceptable playthings. *Photo: Jacquie DeLillo*

The Sick Kitten

What your kitten isn't doing may be the first sign that she is ill. For instance, she may lack energy or seem uninterested in eating. Kittens that lose their appetites, have diarrhea, or act abnormally should be taken to the veterinarian as soon as possible.

Sick kittens run the risk of becoming hypothermic; that is, their temperature may drop below normal. Keep your kitten warm as described in the chapter on first aid. Do not feed a hypothermic kitten until her temperature returns to normal.

This kitten's right eye has been temporarily closed by conjunctivitis, a side effect of an upper respiratory infection. These infections usually clear up with careful treatment.
Photo: Ginger S. Buck

COMMON MEDICAL PROBLEMS

The following information details some of the common medical problems and kitten diseases you may encounter. It is meant as a general guide and should not replace the advice of your veterinarian.

Upper Respiratory Infections

Upper respiratory infections (URIs) are common in orphan kittens rescued from outdoors or kittens that are stressed. URIs are primarily viral in origin but can be caused by a pathogen called chlamydia, which affects a kitten's eyes. A mild URI case resembles the human common cold, complete with sneezing and runny eyes. Mild cases in kittens, however, can quickly turn into more serious conditions. A kitten that stops eating, has difficulty breathing, or develops a yellow-green discharge from

The kitten on the left, though basically healthy, shows the tragic sign of an untreated upper respiratory infection in early kittenhood—blindness in one eye. *Photo: Jacquie DeLillo*

her eyes or nose should be seen by a vet immediately. Severe cases can cause high fever, appetite loss, dehydration, and eye ulcers. Many other diseases stem from URI, and several respiratory diseases cause similar symptoms of coughing, sneezing, and nasal discharge. Probable causes are feline viral rhinotracheitis and feline calicivirus, diseases that can become chronic and sometimes incurable.

URI is highly contagious to other cats and transmitted by contact with infected eye or nasal discharge, airborne droplets, contaminated litter pans, food and water bowls, and your hands and clothing. All kittens with URI should be isolated until the cause and severity of the infection can be assessed by a veterinarian.

Mild cases are treatable by providing a warm, draft-free environment, cleaning eye and nose discharge with a cotton ball moistened with warm water, and using a room vaporizer to ease nasal congestion. A topical decongestant may also be recommended by your veterinarian.

External Parasites

Many, if not most, kittens born outdoors have external parasites that should be removed as soon as possible. While it's a good idea to contact your veterinarian about the safest methods to use for your

HELPFUL HINT!

Conjunctivitis, an inflammation of the membrane lining the eyelids, is a common side effect of upper respiratory infections that often "pastes" the kitten's eyes closed. To help heal the eyes, clean the area with a warm, moistened cotton ball and apply a veterinary-approved eye ointment approximately four times a day or as directed.

Constant scratching may be a sign of fleas, which can be fatal to small kittens. *Photo: Jacquie DeLillo*

particular situation, feline experts have a few suggestions.

Fleas pose a serious health threat to kittens because they can literally suck the blood (and life) from them. While fleas generally aren't life-threatening to adult cats, kittens can die from anemia caused by too many fleas on their small bodies. (Severe anemia from fleas requires a veterinarian's help—kittens with severe anemia may require blood transfusions and intensive nursing care.) It's safe to say that tiny kittens can also die by becoming chilled during a bath to get rid of these parasites.

Fleas are usually visible on kittens—their fur isn't thick enough to hide fleas as they travel around the kitten's body. To remove fleas, start by pulling them off by hand or use a flea comb to gently remove fleas, flea dirt, and flea eggs (which look like grains of salt).

Despite the risk of chilling, it may be necessary to bathe your kitten if she is severely infested.

Before you start, it's a good idea to gather everything you'll need to bathe your kitten, such as towels, washcloths, cotton balls, and cat shampoo. This saves time and helps you observe an important safety rule: Never leave your kitten alone during a bath.

1. Heat the room you will bathe the kitten in to approximately 85° F (29° C) (in other words, nice and warm). Fill a bathroom or kitchen sink with just a few inches of warm water. Test the water temperature on your wrist—if it's comfortable (but not hot) for you, it will be fine for your kitten. Put a small towel or rubber mat in the bottom of the sink to give the kitten something to grip.

2. To prevent water from going into all the wrong places, gently place cotton in the kitten's ears and a veterinarian-approved eye ointment in her eyes.

3. Use only a small amount of a gentle shampoo for cats. Begin washing your kitten at the neck and work toward the tail. Never immerse your kitten's head in water. Instead, gently wash her face with a warm, damp washcloth. You can mimic a mother cat's tongue with short rubs of the cloth.

4. Rinse well with warm, not hot, water until all soap is removed.

5. Wrap your kitten in a warm towel and pat dry.

6. If your kitten seems calm, you can try using a hair dryer set on the lowest heat. Hold it at a safe distance.

7. Make sure your kitten is completely warm and dry before leaving the bathroom.

Warning! *Using flea products, including shampoos, can harm young kittens. Get your vet's advice first.*

Lice feed on the skin scales of kittens and are often found on malnourished kittens. Kitten lice are pale and move slowly. The eggs attach to the kitten's hair shafts and do not easily brush off. This type of lice does not transfer to people. With veterinary approval, carefully follow the bathing instructions suggested in this section to remove kitten lice.

Ear mites look like microscopic spiders and give themselves away when kittens shake their heads, paw, and scratch their ears repeatedly. Another clue to ear mite infestation: Look in the kitten's ear for a brown, waxy material that resembles coffee grounds.

Clean your kitten's ears by moistening a cotton ball with mineral oil. Wrap around your finger and gently wipe the ear surface to remove debris. A cotton swab dabbed with mineral oil can also be used to clean the tiny creases in the ear. Hold the cotton swab vertically and downward to avoid getting dangerously close to the eardrum. Consult your veterinarian for the safest medication to use to kill the ear mites.

Internal Parasites

A host of internal parasites can make themselves at home in your kittens, causing appetite loss, diarrhea, and anemia. Your veterinarian will need to examine a stool sample to prescribe the appropriate medication. A brief description of the most common internal worms and gastro-intestinal parasites is listed below.

Roundworms: A majority of orphan kittens are infested with roundworms, which infect kittens through their mother's milk. You may observe the worms in your kitten's stool.

Basic preventive care for your kitten, including ear cleaning and claw clipping, will keep her healthy and happy. *Photos: Isabelle Francais*

Eyes are bright, shiny, and clear.

Ears are clean and free of discharge.

Nose is clear with no discharge.

Gums are pink (unless naturally pigmented) with no sores or ulcers.

Teeth look clean.

Coat appears shiny, clean, and free of fleas, scabs, and mats.

Genitalia is clean and free of discoloration or dried waste.

Body is soft and smooth; may be on lean side but not skinny (you can feel ribs but not see them); no potbelly.

Tapeworms: You may notice rice-like segments around the kitten's anus. Kittens become infected by ingesting fleas infected with a tapeworm. This internal parasite is not life-threatening but should be treated by a veterinarian.

Hookworms: The stool of a kitten with hookworms looks black and possibly bloody. Hookworms pass to kittens through mother's milk. Potentially deadly, an acute infestation can cause anemia and loss of blood.

Giardia: A protozoan parasite of the small intestinal tract, giardia causes malabsorption of nutrients and results in severe diarrhea. A yellow, foamy stool may indicate this parasite.

Coccidia: Another protozoan parasite affecting the small intestine and the beginning of the large intestine. Coccidia can cause dysentery in kittens. Blood and

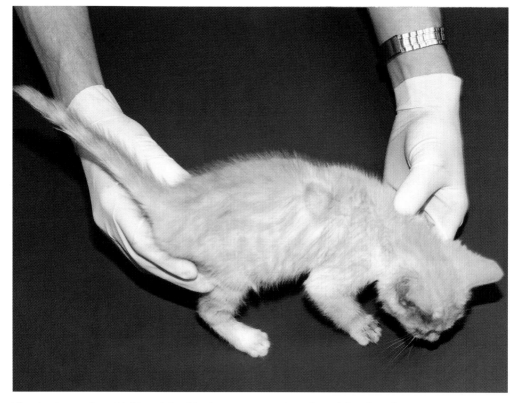

The circular mark on this kitten's back is ringworm, a common fungal skin disorder that is contagious to humans. Treatment is easy with your veterinarian's help. *Photo: Ginger S. Buck*

mucus in the stool are evidence of this life-threatening parasite.

Neonatal Kitten Diseases
Diseases affecting young kittens are listed below. Contact your veterinarian immediately if you suspect your kittens are under the weather.

Panleukopenia (feline distemper) may be contracted before birth. A highly destructive disease, panleukopenia can cause balance and walking problems in kittens beginning at two or three weeks of age.

Feline leukemia virus (FeLV) suppresses the kitten's immune system and may cause "fading kitten" syndrome, in which neonatal kittens weaken and die rapidly. Signs of FeLV include fever, loss of appetite, weight loss, listlessness, and pale mucous membranes. A blood test is required to diagnose this disease.

Feline infectious peritonitis (FIP) is a fatal

disease responsible for a small percentage of kitten deaths. While early signs of this disease are similar to those listed above, a fluctuating fever appears to be typical in cats with FIP.

Ringworm
Ringworm is a common skin disorder of kittens. It's a fungal infection that has nothing to do with worms. Classic signs include circular areas of fur loss or bald patches with scaly skin at the center and an advancing red ring at the circle's rim. Ringworm is highly contagious to people and other animals, so you'll need to consult your veterinarian for help. You can treat a mild case by clipping hair at the edges of the ringworm patch and washing the area with an antifungal shampoo. An antifungal cream or ointment should be applied topically. Be sure to keep the infected kitten away from other pets until she is well, and disinfect the environment to prevent reinfection. Wash your hands with a mild bleach solution, followed by soap and water, after handling the infected kitten.

Taming Feral Kittens

The litter of tiny kittens hidden behind the woodpile looks as precious as any other litter of kittens might, yet as you approach them, they begin to hiss and spit. You've discovered a litter of feral kittens.

Feral cats are, for all intents and purposes, wild. However, they can be tamed if they are captured young enough. Even very young feral kittens may hiss and spit or try to scratch and bite as you approach them. Many orphan

It's never a good idea to capture even very young feral kittens without gloves. Scared kittens will bite and scratch in self-defense. *Photo: Ginger S. Buck*

kittens are the offspring of stray or feral cats, in turn becoming new generations of feral cats themselves. They must be handled a little differently than their tamer relations, but much of the information in this book will still apply to them as well. Many cat lovers claim that feral kittens, once tamed, bond very strongly with those who raise them. I can vouch for this. To become affectionate, loving companions, though, feral kittens need to be pulled out of the repetitive breeding cycle and placed in adoptive homes as early as possible.

APPROACHING FERAL KITTENS

Remember that kittens that try to defend themselves are terrified of you! To a kitten with little or no human contact, people are possible predators—and pretty large ones at that. Feral kittens should not be caught before weaning, or about four weeks of age. Of course, age is a moot point if the tiny, unweaned feral kittens are abandoned or orphaned. In that case, you'll want to follow the procedures for handraising kittens outlined in this book. It's possible to catch feral kittens between four and six weeks of age without using a humane trap, but they may still be too wild to be handled. Never try to capture feral kittens with your bare hands. Instead, wear protective gloves or use a thick towel to pick up the kitten and prevent her escape.

WARNING

All cat bites are potentially serious. If you are bitten, seek medical attention immediately and quarantine the kitten.

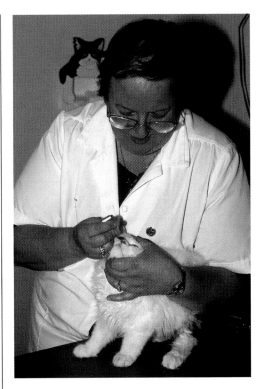

Feral kittens should receive a clean bill of health from a veterinarian and be tested for diseases contagious to other cats before you bring them home. *Photo: Joan Balzarini*

HUMANE TRAPPING

Feral kittens may be captured in humane box traps that can be borrowed from cat rescue groups, humane organizations, or animal shelters. First-time trappers are often shocked at how violently feral cats initially react when they are trapped, so it's a good idea to ask an experienced person what you can expect to encounter. (Alley Cat Allies offers a video that details the humane trapping process; information about the organization follows at the end of this chapter.) If possible, the mother cat should also be captured and spayed to prevent future feral litters.

Feral kittens should receive a clean bill of health from a veterinarian and be tested for diseases contagious to other cats before bringing them home. Keep them separated from other cats in the household at first, and always wash your hands with an antibacterial soap after caring for feral kittens. Wear a smock or other outer clothing that you can shed after you care for the kittens. Taking such precautions can go a long way toward preventing the spread of feline diseases.

THE TAMING PROCESS

Taming feral kittens can take anywhere between two and six weeks or longer, depending on their age and state of wildness, according to the Feral Cat Coalition based in San Diego, California. Kittens are individuals whose temperaments vary greatly, even within the same litter. Taming a feral kitten requires patience, commitment, and lots of love, but the process can be tremendously rewarding.

If you do not have a suitable cage or pet carrier available, confinement in a very small room, such as the bathroom, can also work.
Photo: Wendy Nelson

The steps involved in the taming process are listed below, courtesy of the Feral Cat Coalition.

1. **Containment in a cage or large pet carrier.** Transfer your feral kitten to a cage or a pet carrier large enough for a small litter box and bedding. Place the kitten's new home in a small room away from family pets and children.

The first step in the taming process is to transfer your kitten to a large cage or carrier with food, water, and a litter box. Leave her alone for a few days until she becomes used to your presence.
Photo: Isabelle Francais

HELPFUL HINT!

Don't leave feral kittens in quiet isolation for long periods of time. Let them hear human voices, televisions, and the normal clatter of your household. Walk by your feral kittens' carrier or room often, and talk to them whenever you get the chance during the taming process. You can continue to help your feral kitten adjust to domesticity while you are gone for a few hours—just leave a radio or stereo on and treat your feral kitten to soothing classical or soft pop music.

Do not attempt to handle the kitten for the first two days as she learns to feel safe. Visit her frequently and talk quietly, but resist touching her. Always move slowly around her.

Food and water should be placed in the cage or carrier, along with a small litter box or pan. Many cages have food and water bowls attached to the doors, so that you can feed and water the kittens without placing your hands inside the feral kitten's safe place.

Another method is to place the kittens in a small room, such as a bathroom, in the carrier. Put the litter box in the room and leave the carrier door open so that kittens have access to the box. Remove toxic cleaners, put the toilet seat down, and otherwise kitten-proof the room as needed.

Use some of your worn clothing as bedding for feral kittens. This will help them get used to your scent.

Whichever method you choose, remember to give feral kittens a place they can hide. Something as simple as an overturned box with a small entrance can provide a safe retreat.

2. Periodic and brief handling with a protective towel. After two days, select the least aggressive kitten, place a towel over her, and pick her up in the towel. If the kitten stays calm, pet her gently on the head from behind. Don't approach a kitten from the front; a hand coming directly toward the kitten will frighten her.

After two days, place a towel around the least aggressive kitten and pick her up. If she remains calm, put the towel on your lap and set the kitten on the towel. *Photo: Wendy Nelson*

If the kittens are fairly tame within a week, allow them to have free run of a small room.
Photo: Isabelle Francais

If the kitten remains calm, grip her by the nape of the neck, put the towel on your lap, and set the kitten on the towel. Talk gently to her and stroke her body briefly, then release her.

After handling, reward your kitten with a treat she can lick off a spoon, such as a tiny amount of canned kitten food. Repeat this process often—hand-feeding food is an excellent way to bond with your kittens and speed up taming.

Begin to brush your kitten with a soft pet brush to mimic a mother cat's grooming, and work your way up to using a flea comb. Talk to her often. The attention will give your kitten a feeling of well-being, and she will begin to transfer her need for maternal love to you.

Do not stare at your kittens for any length of time. Cats consider this to be a form of aggressive body language. Instead, avert your eyes and lower your head often to signal submissive, friendly behavior.

You can begin to play with your kitten now. Choose "kitty tease" toys or other lightweight cat toys, but be sure not to leave string toys with a feral kitten that may try to eat the string while you are gone.

3. Containment in a small room. If your kitten has made considerable progress within a week, she should be allowed access to a small room and should be placed in the cage only if needed. A large room may overwhelm a timid kitten and increase her fear level. For example, bedrooms may not be a good choice if the kitten hides under the bed and you have difficulty reaching her.

In fact, the tiny places and spaces a kitten can wedge into in any room will amaze you. Think like a kitten by getting down on her level; then kitten-proof her quarters as much as possible. Resist the impulse to chase her if she begins to head somewhere you don't want her to go—chasing will reinforce her already-ingrained urge to run from you. Even very tame, former feral cats can develop the habit of fleeing from the people they love if they are chased during the training period.

4. Exposure to other people. When the kittens no longer respond by scratching or biting, you can encourage friends to handle them frequently. Feral cats tend to bond with one person, so it's a good idea to socialize them with other people and children who are willing to handle the kittens quietly.

5. Placement in suitable adoptive homes. Feral kittens can be adopted out at approximately eight weeks of age if they are tamed and socialized to people. The most suitable home is a calm environment in which the kittens will feel safe and secure. A perfect home for feral cats is two feral cats kept indoors! Ensure that the kitten is spayed or neutered, either before or after adoption.

FERAL CAT RESOURCES

Alley Cat Allies
1801 Belmont Road NW, #201
Washington, DC 20009
(202) 667-3630
www.alleycat.org

Feral Cat Coalition
9528 Miramar Road #160
San Diego, CA 92126
(619) 497-1599
www.feralcat.com

Letting Go of the Orphan Kitten

Foster parents know the toughest part of raising orphan kittens is often letting them go to new homes. It's natural to feel both happy and a little sad during this time. Handraising orphan kittens is a personal journey, and it is easy to become emotionally attached to them. The deep bond created in helping a tiny kitten fight for life will stay with you, perhaps always.

There are many ways to find homes for your orphan kittens. Some foster parents develop good relationships with local shelters that can help adopt the kittens out in exchange for donations or volunteer work.

The toughest part of raising orphan kittens is letting them go to new homes. It's easy to become attached to the cuties whose lives you saved. *Photo: John Tyson*

There is no reason to wait the traditional eight to ten weeks to place your foster kittens in new homes, as long as they are weaned and socialized.
Photo: Beverly Adams

You may choose to keep the orphans you raise permanently, of course, but if that isn't possible, decide early on that you are fostering kittens that will be placed in other homes. When the time comes, it will help make the adjustment a little bit easier.

PUT THE WORD OUT

It's wise to circulate the news about the kittens' adoption availability early on. Putting the word out can mean anything from placing an ad in local papers and posting a notice at your veterinary hospital or pet supply store to letting all your cat-loving friends know you have the cutest kittens in town. Be sure to charge at least a small fee for your kitten's adoption, because kittens that are offered "free to good home" may not always land in one. Responsible pet owners will not mind paying an adoption fee if you explain that it covers many veterinary services that you have already taken care of, such as vaccinations and disease testing. (Of course, it's okay not to charge an adoption fee to someone you know very well and trust.) Screen potential adopters carefully, especially if you have strong feelings about declawing or keeping your kitten an indoor-only cat. You also may want to visit your kitten's potential new home or ask where your kitten will be receiving veterinary care.

Foster kittens are not in a normal situation, so there is no reason to wait the traditional eight to ten weeks to adopt them out. This especially holds true for single kittens that have no littermates or mother cats to continue socializing them. If you find a caring person who is willing to take up where you leave off, you can adopt your kittens out at as early as five to six weeks old. Be sure to pass along copies of the kitten's veterinary records and show the new owner how to care for the kitten. Explain that you will be glad to be a resource for that person to answer questions or provide help during the transition process. To give you a little more peace of mind and provide your kitten with additional protection, you might also want to add that if for any reason the adoption does not work out, the kitten should be returned to you.

SPAY OR NEUTER

If at all possible, spay or neuter your kittens before placing them in adoptive homes. Many animal welfare organizations and a growing number of veterinarians now advocate spaying and neutering kittens as young as eight weeks of age. Alley Cat Allies suggests that cat owners and foster parents should not contribute to the cat overpopulation problem in any way by allowing unaltered cats to be placed in homes.

Early spay/neuter may not be an affordable or timely option for you at the time of your kittens' adoption, so do the next best thing. Insist that your kittens be spayed or neutered by their new owners as soon as possible. Put it in writing by devising a simple adoption contract like the sample at the back of this book to ensure the health and well-being of your kittens. For example, the contract might state that the new pet owners agree to vaccinate and spay or neuter the kitten by an agreed-upon date. The contract also may stipulate that the kitten be returned to you if for any reason the new caretakers decide not to keep her. Then, go the extra mile by following up on the agreement. It's the least you can do to help guarantee your beautiful orphan kitten a long and happy future.

HELPFUL HINT!

Give your kitten some added protection during the transition to her new home. Send her off with a brand new collar and identifying information, and provide a coupon or gift certificate to encourage your kitten's new guardian to purchase a new identification tag soon.

Send your kitten to her new home in a safe plastic carrier along with a collar and ID tag for extra security.
Photo: Isabelle Francais

Appendix

WEIGHT CHART				
Date	Weight	Gain	Loss	Notes
				(Please initial your entries)

The helpful charts on pages 60-62 are reprinted courtesy of Alley Cat Allies.

FEEDING SCHEDULE				Kitten's Name:	
Date	Time	AM	PM	Amount	Notes
					(Please initial your entries)

PROGRESS REPORT

Kitten's Name:

Date	Time	General Appearance			Appetite		Weight			Elimination - Feces		Notes
		Good	Guarded	Poor	Good	Poor	Gain	Loss	Normal	Diarrhea		(Please initial your entries)

CAT ADOPTION CONTRACT

Name_____

Address_____

City_____State_____Zip_____

Home Phone_____ Work Phone_____

Driver's License #_____

I would like to adopt_____
                        (Kitten's name, age, description)

As a responsible pet owner, I agree to the following terms:

1) I will spay/neuter my kitten by_____.
                                    (Date)

2) I will maintain my new pet's health and well-being by providing adequate food, fresh
water, veterinary care, and vaccinations upon the recommendation of my veterinarian

_____.

 (Veterinarian's name)

3) I understand that my kitten should be kept indoors and should not be declawed.

4) I agree to provide my cat with current identifying information, such as a
collar/tag and microchip I.D.

5) If, for any reason, I decide not to keep this cat, I agree to return him/her to

_____.

_____

(Signature)   (Date)

**This sample adoption contract will help you format one to fit your own needs. Make sure to keep a copy
for yourself and give one to the adopters.**

Index

Page numbers in **bold** indicate photos

Academy of Feline Medicine 17
Adoption contract .... 59, 63 (sample)
Adoption fee, importance of 58
Alley Cat Allies 11, 19, 49, 51, 55, 59, 60
American Association of Feline
   Practitioners 17
Anemia 46
ASPCA, "From Kitten to Cat" 34
Bathing a kitten 46
Bottle-feeding 25-27, **26**
Bruce, Annie 41
Building a nest 8
Burping a kitten 26, **28**
Cat Be Good 41
Cat Fancy 15
Children and kittens 34
Chilling, dangers of 7
Choking during feeding 28
Cleaning the nest 10
Coccidia 48
Colostrum 10, 21, 49
Conjunctivitis **44**, 45
Cow's milk 21
Dehydration, detection and prevention of 11
Determining orphan status of kittens 7
Ear mites 47
Ears, cleaning 47
Elimination, stimulating 29
Emergency checklist 8
Eyedropper-feeding 27
Feeding chart 22
Feeding devices **24**
Feeding do's and don'ts 32
Feeding schedule (sample) 61
Feline infectious peritonitis (FIP) 49
Feline leukemia virus (FeLV) 49
Feral Cat Coalition 52, 55
Finding homes for kittens 60
First aid 6
Fleas 46
Foster mothers, locating 13
Giardia 48
Grieving a loss 5, 17
Growth and development of
   newborn kittens 18-21
      8 hours old **18**
      6 days old **19**
      12 days old **20**
      2 1/2 weeks old **20**
      3 weeks old **20**
      4 1/2 weeks old **21**
      17 weeks old **21**

Hand-feeding kittens 18
Handling, importance of 34, 36
Health care 44
Healthy kitten, signs of 48
Heating pads 9
Homeless Cat Network 25
Homemade formulas 22, 25
Hookworms 48
Humane trapping 51
Hypothermia 7, 44
Infrared heating light 9
Introducing kittens to a foster mother 14
Isolation, importance of 10
Lice 46
Litter box training 33
Milk replacer formulas 21, **23**
Overfeeding vs. underfeeding 22
Panleukopenia (feline distemper) 49
Parasites, external 45
Parasites, internal 47
Picking up a kitten 37
Progress report (sample) 62
Props to keep the single kitten company 40, **41**
Record-keeping 11
Ringworm **48**, 49
Roundworms 47
Rumberger, Deborah 15
Sex, determining 21
Shelters and orphan kittens 14
Single kittens, special needs of 9, 38
Socializing the single kitten 41-42
Socializing 34
Solid food, introducing 31
Spaying/neutering 59
Supplies needed to handraise kittens 7
Taming feral kittens 50
Tapeworms 48
Temperature, average of a newborn kitten 7
Temperature, environmental 9
Temperature, how to take 8
Tube-feeding 27-28
Upper respiratory infections 44-45
Vaccination schedule 17, 21, 49
Veterinarian, importance of 5, 11, 15, 17
Warming a chilled kitten 8
Warmth, importance of 7, 38
Washing after feedings 29
Water 31
Weaning 30
Weighing kittens 18
Weight chart .... 19, 60 (sample)
Weight gain, typical 18